Brand Vinci
Decoding facets of branding

BRAND VINCI

Decoding facets of branding

PAVAN PADAKI

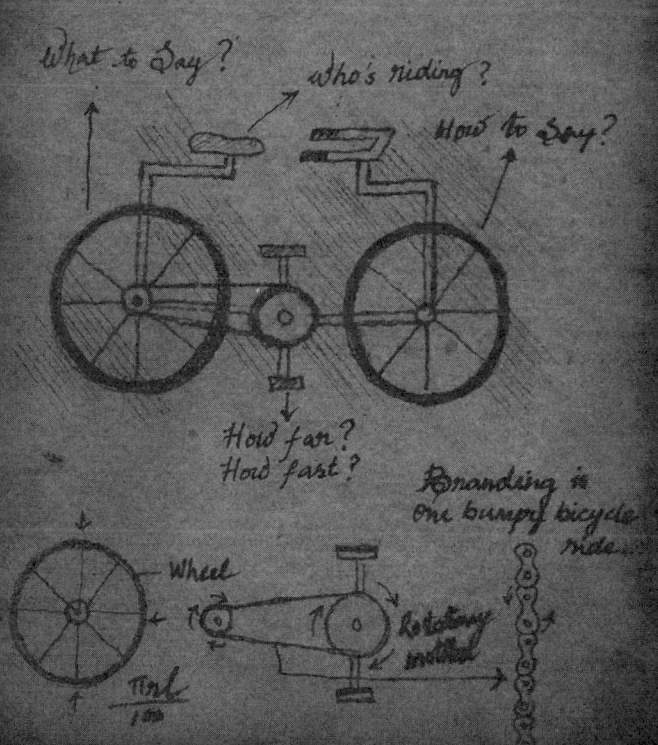

Bloomsbury Publishing India Pvt Ltd
Vishrut Building, DDA Complex
Building No. 3, Pocket C-6 & 7, Vasant Kunj
New Delhi 110 070

ISBN: 978-93-84052-68-3
10 9 8 7 6 5 4 3 2 1

Typeset by Eleven Arts
Printed and bound by Thomson Press India Ltd

To my father, Bindu Padaki,
whose thinking and ideas were
always ahead of his time

Contents

Acknowledgements

Little did I realise that my hobby would eventually become my career. This is my 25th year in the business of advertising and branding. Looking back, it seems, there is a default logic to it. I thank my father for exposing me to over a 1,000 comics; a 100 MAD magazines; 200 satellite channels in the early 80's; music loaded on over 300 spools; 200 LP vinyl records; 400 cassette tapes; 200 VHS movies, and TV shows from across an array of countries; and for championing my unique hobby of collecting TV commercials from across the globe. Even before I had stepped into the world of advertising,I had over 1,000 TV commercials and radio spots.

To Sridhar, my colleague, well-wisher, and the CEO of brand-comm, who has always believed that I can, and will deliver the best, and succeed. I would like to acknowledge, and express my gratitude for him, for supporting and helping me discover the multiple facets of branding and communication. For my first TV script, first pitch presentation, first speaking opportunity, first workshop as a trainer, first brand consulting project, first B-school lecture, and many other firsts, thank you! Today, I take pleasure in expressing my insights on branding.

I would also express my heartfelt gratitude to all my colleagues and well-wishers, for encouraging me to write this book. Special thanks to Parvarthy, Gasper, and Saloni, for their support and energy in making this book a reality. Thanks to Chatura and Ashok for minding my language, and Benjamin for those wonderful hand-sketched DaVinci images.

I thank Praveen Tiwari, Publisher, Bloomsbury India, for his support, confidence, and conviction in the book.

To my clients, workshop participants, and B-school students, who have contributed richly to my knowledge and experience, and have helped me unlearn, to become a professional brand practitioner.

Thank you all!

Foreword

R. Balki: Chairman, Lowe Lintas; writer, director, producer (Cheeni Kum; Paa; English Vinglish)

This is possibly the first forget-me-not book on brands. It is for all of us; students, practitioners, and teachers, who sometimes forget that a brand is as human as us.

In a competitive world, where all of us are desperately trying to be brands ourselves, it is forgivable when we sometimes forget to look at a brand, as if it were a person. But it is unforgivable if we don't quickly correct this. Pavan's book is a gentle delight that tells students how to treat brands, remind practitioners how to continue treating brands, and refreshes teachers with new brand lessons.

Pavan has removed all jargons that cloud the understanding of brands. It is a book written by a practitioner who has treated brands all his life with an understanding that some of us reserve only for a close friend or family. Maybe that is why the book is a pleasant nudge, and not a missionary lecture.

Life is very connected. Sometimes doing things for a brand actually improves our understanding of fellow humans. After all, the rules are the same.

I strongly advise all communicators to read this book, and keep it in a place, close to them, in case of an emergency.

Balki

Author's Note

This book is an attempt to express the various facets of branding, based on hearsay, industry experience, interactions at corporate meetings, workshop interactions, and personal memories. This is to inspire and help the reader appreciate key facets of branding, and treat the references provided as illustrative examples, which would allow her/him to reflect upon brands that s/he is engaged with.

How to use the decoded facets:

1. Read each facet once, in sequence, and study the simplicity around the facet to appreciate its impact on a brand.

2. Read individual facets once again, and test your brand in the context of the facet being decoded, by asking yourself the following:

   a) How would my brand articulate or play itself out on this particular brand facet?

   b) Could this facet be the missing link for my brand as of today?

   c) If I were to start strategising with a fresh approach, which of these facets in combination, could dramatically change the status of my brand?

   d) What if my competitor uses these decoded facets in his favour, or against my brand?

I am confident that many would benefit, by applying these brand facets to their personal lives as well; because I believe, brands too have lives like us.

Preface

Welcome to the world of brands, which we all hear so much about, and deal with, almost every second of our lives. Welcome to a world where brands and branding have been drained out of common sense, making them unnecessarily complex, highly intellectual, and boringly academic.

Here is a book with a 'brand sense', that attempts to decode the very design of branding as a concept, and as a tool. We look at its relevance in our daily lives, with the belief, that it is part of our lives as a basic instinct. It seems strange, that even Leonardo da Vinci, a legendary painter, sculptor, architect, musician, scientist, mathematician, engineer, inventor, anatomist, geologist, cartographer, botanist and a writer, did not explore the world of brands as a subject. Or, is it possible that his work on brands and branding is still a well-kept secret?

This decoded book on brands is for all those who know what the facets of a brand mean; but do not know what they are. The book explores some key aspects, which form the genesis of brands beyond jargons and clichéd usage for the sake of impressive 'brand conversations', and beyond the constant ramble during meetings.

Branding has been branded as an art form by some, while many term it as science. So before we dwell over all the jargons churned out on a daily basis, here are some brand facets to be acknowledged as basic instincts—Brand Purpose; Brand Perspective; Brand Positioning and Repositioning; and Brand Protocol.

Trust this book will help simplify some of the complexities around the word 'brands', and make 'brand sense' for our daily lives.

Maybe it is not a secret anymore, Da Vinci.

FACET I

First things First

Brand Balance

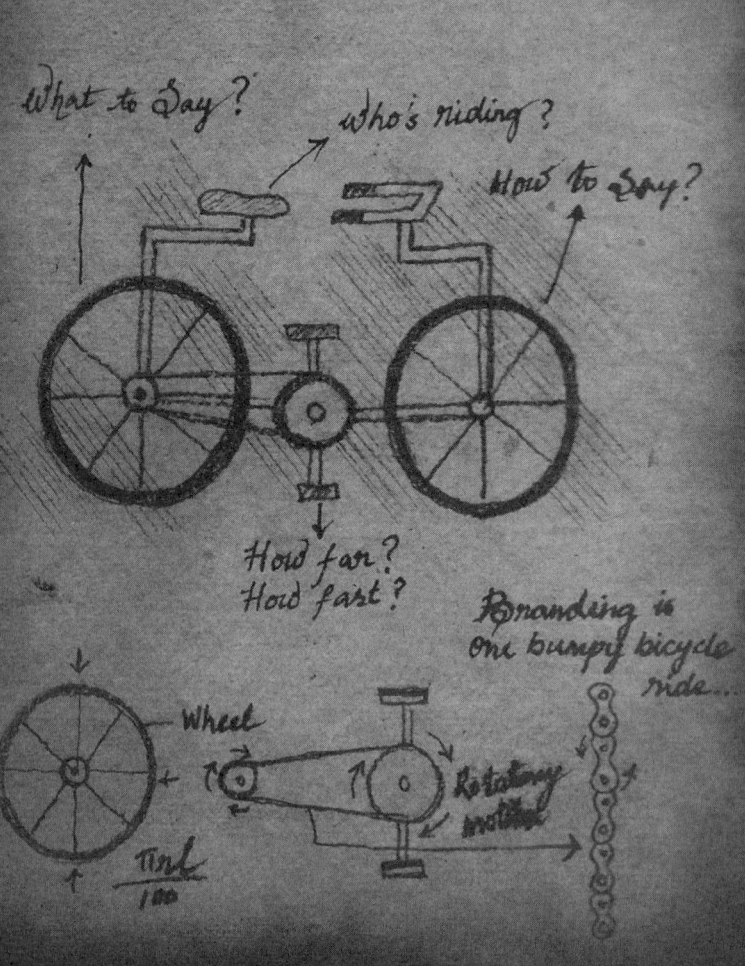

What to Say?

Who's riding?

How to Say?

How far?
How fast?

Branding is one bumpy bicycle ride...

Wheel

Tint
100

Rotating motion

First things First
Brand Balance

Here is the secret; grasp this, and you will never have to fear the big brand books on library shelves, or feel inadequate when brand gurus speak to you at seminars and lectures.

I have come to realise, or should I say, decoded, the universal truth, that brands have lives, and live like humans. Much like humans, they believe they are clear about their lives sometimes, confused most of the times, and anxious all the time; because, life is like a bumpy bicycle ride.

Your energy and resources will determine how much, and how to, crank the pedal.

Decoding the basis of the lives of brands, resulted into deciphering, that it is a journey to determine how far you wish to, and how fast you aim to go. Your conviction, your motivation, your energy, and resources, will determine how much, and how to, crank the pedal, and for how long, and with how much effort. This, only time and situations could unfold.

Let us now begin to decode further, the core aspects of brands (or life).

There are two wheels that need to be balanced. They are not mutually exclusive, and are highly interdependent; the balance between 'what to say?' and 'how to say it?'

 Decoding 'what to say?'

This is about determining the 'strategy'. Simply put, this means making choices, and taking a call.

'What to say?' determines and harmonises your brand purpose, brand positioning, brand perspective, brand properties, and brand

Brand Links

brand protocal

brand properties

brand positioning

brand purpose

brand perspective

protocol. Don't worry; these are decoded for you in the subsequent chapters! This book decodes all these facets of 'what to say?'

It takes into account the legacy of the brand custodian or the creator's intentions, resources, wisdom, and experience, and above all, the product or service, and its relevance in the market, vis à-vis its competition and end-user needs.

 ### Decoding 'how to say it?'

This is about expressing, communicating, and reaching the pre-determined 'what to say?' to your intended audiences. In other words, it means how to execute the 'what to say?' (the strategy).

'How to say it?' expresses the brand perspective, brand positioning, and brand personality in multiple ways. The expression can be executed in the form of a brand name, identity, packaging, advertising, public relations, events, mailers, in-film placements, social media, and so on.

The strategic choices of 'how to say it?' stem from achieving clarity of 'what to say?'.

In other words, you could call it creative strategy and execution.

 **Decoding 'where to go?'**

This is about steering the brand into different markets, or re-positioning (if need be), and redefining its audiences its proposition, its personality, marketing budgets, etc. It simply means keeping the brand on course.

In an ever-changing world of brands, consumer behaviours are bound to constantly change as well, since there is a constant influx of new ideas and new needs. Aspirations and expectations keep changing, as do cultural and established habits, redefining the value system itself.

The brand custodian or the creator, needs to be proactive to steer the brand, and determine the 'where to go?'

 Decoding 'who's riding?'

This is about understanding and reflecting on the brand custodian's, or the creator's ambition, desire, and purpose for the brand. Identifying whether the ride is for a personal objective, a social objective, or an objective to simply continue a legacy, will help the brand balance itself.

Many a times, a business objective would dominate and overshadow the genesis of the brand. The ride would then become bumpy, resulting in the rider to constantly check the course, consuming precious time and resources.

Every time the brand custodian feels that the brand balance is becoming a challenge, it would help to check the brand purpose first.

The subsequent chapters decode some of the other core brand facets of 'what to say?'.

FACET II

It's purpose first, business next!

Brand Purpose

Why should I exist in the future?

why should I exist today?

Determining the brand purpose directs you to move in a particular direction.
Connects people...
Inspires people...

It's purpose first, business next!

Brand Purpose

It is true that brands have lives and live lives like humans; and yet, there is one crucial difference. We humans live our lives, desperately trying to discover its purpose. Many seek out life gurus, or take a trip to the Himalayas to discover the purpose of life. It's almost as if not knowing that well-kept secret, which prevents us from really 'living'.

But brands, on the other hand, are created by us humans, and we need to determine and define the purpose of the brand that we create.

The secret lies with us. The amusing thing is, that sometimes we, the creators or custodians of brands, tend to forget the purpose of the brand we create. The journey, then, is bound to be a big bumpy ride. No wonder 'brand gurus' are in demand!

It's simple actually. The secret to a brand's purpose will be clear if you ask two simple questions:

1. Why should the brand exist today?

2. Why should the brand exist in the future?

Try answering them. While they may sound simple, they are actually difficult to answer. We humans are often overambitious, and sometimes, quite greedy. In the pursuit to get better returns, more returns, or simply trying to demonstrate one-upmanship, the brand purpose gets lost. You got it right! Even brands have egos which cloud their purpose.

Here is a battery of questions which could help you articulate your brand purpose:

Even brands

have egos

which cloud their

purpose.

1. Why should someone work with you or work for you?

2. Why should someone buy from you?

3. Why should someone respect you?

4. Why should someone keep coming back to you?

5. Why should someone talk about you, or share ideas and opinions about you?

Gaining or improving brand awareness, brand recognition, brand loyalty, brand growth, etc., cannot be the brand purpose. They are the fundamental requirements of a brand, for any brand. When you say 'brand', it is an innate desire for the brand to have an identity, which seeks to create better awareness, recognition, and growth. Gaining or improvising them is tactical in nature, and does not define the brand's purpose.

Determining the brand purpose directs you to move in a particular direction. It connects people internally and externally with a definite

A purpose

statement is only as
good as what you
believe, and depends
on how you say it.

purpose. It inspires people, keeps people on track, and also helps people organise the brand.

Knowing or determining the brand purpose is not merely about having clarity on what needs to be done. It brings purpose to not only the brand's user, but also within the organization or the company. Every individual gets to know why s/he comes to the office or factory they work at, and understands what is expected of them every day. It acts like an everyday-appraisal, and constantly enables them to evaluate, if all ideas and actions are in line with the purpose or not.

Before we get down to looking at some examples, it is important to understand that a purpose statement is only as good as what you believe, and depends on how you say it. If the purpose statement lacks passion or conviction, it is bound to show up, sooner or later. It is equally important to determine how the purpose statement expresses itself.

The purpose can be expressed in many ways, without necessarily stating it as a purpose statement. It could get expressed in many forms—as a vision-mission statement, a motto line, a tagline, a positioning statement, a boiler template, etc. Eventually, it will dictate what the brand does, and how it does it, and what it strives to celebrate as an achievement.

Recently, a real estate client showed me the corporate brochure of another realty company, and their mission statement read:

'To delight our customers with quality construction, executed with high degree of professionalism'.

'Delighting customers' and 'quality construction' are basic expectations from a realty company, and my client wondered how the statement could ever inspire anyone internally or externally. Interestingly, the statement made him ponder over the possibility of substandard construction material being used. If not for the declared statement, the quality aspect would not have come under question.

Purpose statements, in any form of expression,

Keeping the purpose statement simple and inspiring can become memorable, enabling a highly productive engagement.

are not meant to be feel-good statements to adorn corporate lobby walls, or as a fill-in for corporate websites. Keeping the purpose statement simple and inspiring can become memorable, enabling a highly productive engagement between the company, its employees, and all the stakeholders, vendors, influencers, and brand champions.

Look at any photograph of Disneyland around the world. Not surprisingly, you will often see as many, or more adults, as children. The reason, I believe, is rooted in its purpose statement. 'Keeping alive the magic of childhood.' It simply means, that if there is a child in you, then you are going to have a great time. This is not by default, but by design, rooted in its purpose statement.

A well-crafted purpose statement can provide the focus and motivation to your business, as the Starbucks mission statement does, which says—'To inspire and nurture the human spirit, one person, one cup and one neighbourhood at a time'.

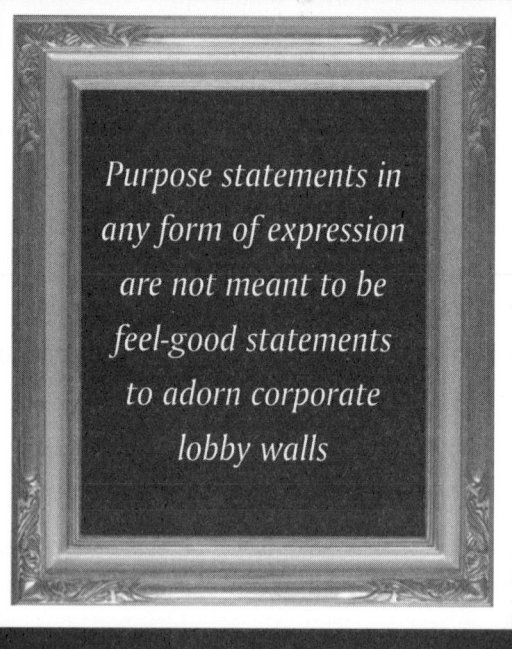

Purpose statements in any form of expression are not meant to be feel-good statements to adorn corporate lobby walls

In retrospect, you will find a well-articulated purpose statement in all well-built legendary brands; and you will also find them to be consistent, clear, and compelling, because of their conviction in their purpose. All marketing, communication, and consumer engagement activities will be based on this.

Even today, you will find Coca-Cola's growth, leadership, sustainability, and its marketing and communication engagements, stemming from its mission statement, which reads—'At The Coca-Cola Company, we strive to refresh the world, inspire moments of optimism and happiness, create value, and make a difference'.

If you look at another iconic brand, Google, you will find that everything they do today, whether it's their search engine, YouTube, Google Play, Maps, Gmail, or news delivery, is because of the clarity in with its purpose. Their mission is simple and relevant with a universal purpose—'To organise the world's information, and make it universally accessible and useful'.

Another way to observe the power of a purpose statement is to always see it from an end-consumer's point of view, examine what need is being addressed, and how. The clarity of eBay about its domain and a universal consumer need, is captured in its purpose statement as— 'To provide a global trading platform, where practically anyone can trade, practically anything'.

Speaking of needs, it is worth noting Mother Teresa's Missionaries of Charity's vow—'To give, wholehearted and free service to the poorest of the poor'. The clarity of its purpose, its end need, and the manner in which it shall fulfil its purpose is single-minded and consistent even today, which makes for a strong and enduring brand.

And now, here is the secret behind all these expressions of purpose. All of them acknowledge and address a human purpose. At the end of the day, brands engage with human needs and emotions. It's time we called them 'humansumer,' rather than 'consumer'.

Brands, in the context of humansumers, have two fundamental roles, which are cardinal. One is to make the unfamiliar familiar, i.e., reinforce an existing perspective; and the other is to present the most familiar with a fresh perspective.

A highly complex technology called a processor, is made familiar, when it is branded and communicated as an Intel Core Processor; or a mobile technology platform is made familiar, when it is branded as Android. A highly familiar portable audio player can be presented with a fresh perspective, as an iPod.

In the next chapter, you will find the power of 'brand perspectives' decoded.

It's time we called them 'humansumers' rather than 'consumer'.

FACET III

Oh! Like that?

Brand Perspective

Relevance

Actual

R-Factor

Only a small alteration
in the refractive angle
A whole new perspective,
highly relevant, highly Impactful.

Oh! Like That?

Brand Perspective

Over the years, eager to coin more smart sounding terminologies and jargons, a cardinal facet called 'brand perspective' seems to have been ignored, having perhaps been considered too elementary. But the secret of a successful brand begins with this. It is like deciding whether it will be a boy or a girl, much before conception. Giving birth and parenting would take its own direction thereafter.

Perspective, as the word suggests, is the art of drawing, so as to give effect of solidity

It is an art; it is subjective; it is relative, and when the relevance is cracked, a brand is born in the eyes of the 'humansumer'.

and relative position and size (reference: Oxford dictionary).

In the context of branding, it means the same. It is an art; it is subjective; it is relative; and when the relevance is cracked, a brand is born in the eyes of the *'humansumer'*.

It is important to determine in whose perspective the brand should be presented, and the perspective that would deliver maximum relevance and impact. Here is a simple story to understand the impact of a perspective.

Once upon a time, there was a baby mosquito, about to take its maiden flight. The anxious parents cautioned the baby mosquito, as it took wings  into the world outside. After several hours, the baby mosquito returned overjoyed, much to the surprise of its parents. When they asked about its flight, the baby mosquito quipped, 'It's a wonderful world out there pa. People were so happy to see me, that they were clapping their hands for me!' Now, that was the baby mosquito's

Market Atmosphere

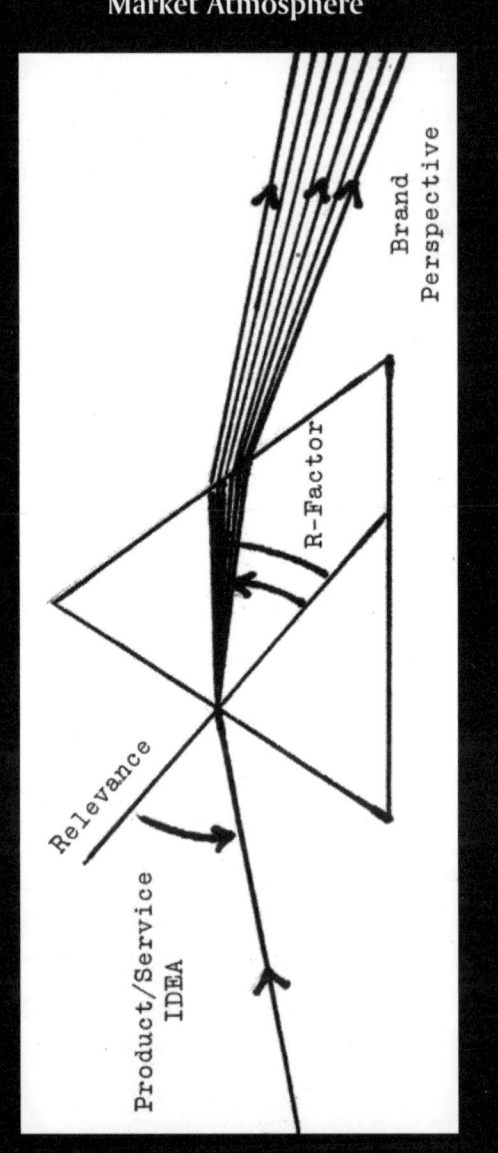

perspective. From your perspective, it was a joke, and from the mosquito's parents' perspective, it was shocking.

Now, let us begin to decode 'brand perspective'. The secret to unveiling a brand perspective is not to reflect on what a product or service is. Pass the product or service idea through a medium called *'market atmosphere'*, and then engineer a refraction, by determining the angle. This angle is the angle of relevance, and the slightest of bends occurring due to the brand refraction could result in a perspective that is fresh and dramatic.

Now, let us decode a crucial aspect called the *'relevance factor'* or the 'R' factor. Nothing is as vital as the relevance factor for the product or service in the eyes of the end-consumer. The relevance factor can be drawn from a wide range of aspects, whether from the past experience, present perceptions, or future trends. It can tap into cultural, behavioural, attitudinal or habitual practices and beliefs, and also examine emotional and aspirational needs.

In addition, insights too play a huge role in determining the refractive angle called 'perspective'.

Let's observe some examples of how a brand perspective has helped position and pitch colas in the market. Cola, in its product form, could be described as a coloured, carbonated sugar drink, with a distinct taste. But, by changing the refractive angle or the 'R' factor, the following distinct positioning is possible:

1. Cola as a refreshing drink.

2. Cola as a cough syrup (I am sure you know what I am referring to. If you don't, check what they have to say about Coca-Cola).

3. Cola as a happiness drink.

4. Cola as a macho drink.

5. Cola as the choice of the new generation, and so on.

The determination of the 'R' factor is highly dependent on the *market atmosphere* at a given point in time, because the *relevance factor* keeps changing with dynamic human needs, both emotionally and functionally.

Let us now observe some brand perspectives from the footwear industry. Footwear, which serves the function of protecting your feet, is being distinctly positioned in the market by taking into account the *'R' factor*, and slightly altering the refractive angle, to result into the birth of some enduring brands.

1. Shoes with an attitude

2. Shoes for the adventurer in you

3. Shoes that celebrate the athlete in you

4. Shoes that last a lifetime

5. Shoes that can take you far

6. Shoes that acknowledge the endurance in you

You will see that all of them are insightful, with only a small alteration in their refractive angle, to give you a whole new perspective; highly relevant and highly impactful.

I always wondered why Tom and Jerry cartoons on TV get away

as entertainment for kids. I strongly feel it needs a PG rating, or an 'A' certificate from the censor board. They exhibit high levels of violence, torture, revenge, and scheming, episode after episode. But, this is merely a perspective. The creators have taken the *'R' factor* as entertainment  and fun for kids. The result—they are the most popular entertainers for children on television, across the globe.

That's what I call the power of a brand perspective.

A brand's positioning will only be as good as its brand perspective. The importance of a brand perspective is usually taken for granted. View it as a strategy, and practice it as an art. Why? Because brand perspective forms the very basis of defining a brand's positioning stance.

A brand's

positioning will

only be as good as

its brand perspective.

FACET IV

Yeah, yeah, I know!

Brand Positioning

(By Un-positioning)

Man

You gain a posdtion at the
Cost of another occupied
position.
It's all in the mind.

Short man

Tall man

Yeah, yeah, I know!

Brand Positioning
(By Un-positioning)

We all know brand positioning as a terminology or jargon, right? At least, most of us believe we know it. It is expressed in many ways as a brand differentiator, the USP, brand proposition, etc. With due acknowledgment and respect to Al Ries and Jean-Noel Kapferer, let us begin to decode brand positioning.

True, brand positioning is about owning a clear differentiator in the minds of the consumers. But, let us examine what really happens in the minds of the consumers. Brand

Positioning and
Un-positioning for an Apple

positioning happens as a result of un-positioning the competition. It is always relative to what is already out there as another equivalent brand, or a substitute product; within or outside the category.

A fruit, when it is recognised as an apple, is still a commodity, yet to be branded. When you identify it as a red apple, it becomes a brand in the context of, say, green apples. When the red apple is presented as a red healthy apple, the red apple begins its attempt to own a thought in the minds of the consumer as a red, healthy apple. Now, going a step further, to ensure that it is not just a healthy apple like the green ones, the red apple could declare itself as 'red healthy apple with no worms.' The result is that, the green apples get un-positioned automatically as apples with worms, without the green apple saying so, allowing the red apple to position itself with a differentiator.

This also illustrates how you are, all the time being un-positioned, without your permission, or many times without your knowledge.

Positioning and
Un-positioning of a juice shop

The competition keeps defining your brand position. In other words, the strength of your brand's positioning is only as good as your un-positioning of the competition.

Let's look at another scenario to understand the power of positioning or un-positioning. A young entrepreneur opened a juice shop around the corner near my office, with a sign board, which read, 'Juice Shop'. A juice shop was born. We, at our office, started referring to it as the 'around the corner juice shop'. A few weeks later, another juice shop opened on the same road with a sign board reading, 'Juice Joint—Healthy and Natural'. Yes, you got it right. The juice shop around the corner got un-positioned automatically, without any reference to his shop directly.

If the decoded brand facet is not clear yet, just stay with me for the next two pages.

There are three fundamental aspects that we need to understand as a framework to brand positioning, which are:

1. The very concept of brand is in the context of the competition and the target audience.

It is a thought or
an idea in the mind
first, and the existence
of the product
thereafter.

2. What you want your target audience to have in their mind, is based on a pre-determined brand position, and what you want to own in their mind can be an idea, a thought, a perspective, a feature, an aspiration, an emotion, etc.

3. As an end-result, your target audience needs to prefer, or accept you as a substitute for their current brand of choice, or as a substitute for a product or service itself, within or outside the category.

You gain a position at the cost of another occupied position.

As explained by Al Ries, positioning happens in the mind. In many ways, it is a thought or an idea in the mind first, with the existence of the product being secondary. How you make your consumers see you is all in the mind. Here again, it is by un-positioning. Now, I am about to reveal the secret of positioning in your mind, or your consumer's mind.

The mind is the mother of all supermarkets. Imagine, in this supermarket, which is your mind,

The Mind
'Mother of all super markets'

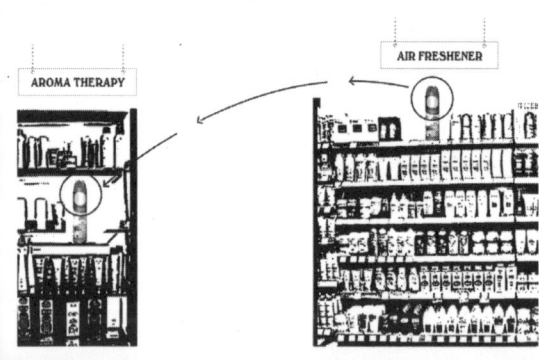

there are multiple levels, aisles, and shelves, all labelled and categorised by a thought, an idea, a descriptor, an attribute, etc. If a can of air freshener on a shelf, labelled as 'air freshener', is taken (remember, the shelf is in your mind), and moved across the opposite aisle to a shelf labeled 'aroma therapy', the air freshener is now positioned in your mind as an aroma therapy spray for relaxing, vis-à-vis an air freshener; thereby un-positioning the air freshener.

In other words, the labelled shelf in your mind or the consumers' minds is a result of un-positioning a particular competitive brand, a substitute product or service.

Here are two more aspects to be decoded. One, you should always re-position your brand as a tactical move to draw better relevance and perspective. You always re-position your brand, and un-position competition or a substitute product or service.

And two, even when you own a fresh thought or an idea, never presented or captured

*The trick is to
determine a relevant
brand perspective,
un-position an existing
brand, product,
or service*

before, you are actually un-positioning an old or an existing idea or thought. Let's take a quick look at some obvious examples around, where a fresh idea un-positioned an existing idea. Mobile phones un-positioned landline phones; eBay un-positioned the weekly auction houses; Google un-positioned the encyclopedia; vacuum cleaners un-positioned domestic help; chocolates and toys un-positioned guilt.

When you take a positioning stance, such as a macho cola, it is only a brand perspective, yet to be established as brand positioning.

Positioning does not happen suddenly; you have to make it happen. A particular positioning stance is only a stance taken, but not established. It takes effort, time, and resources to own a positioning stance. Positioning is said to be in place only when the consumer interprets or decodes it, and holds the thought or the idea in his mind. Here again, a macho cola is positioned by un-positioning other colas as not being macho, making the stance unique.

The trick is to determine a relevant brand perspective, un-position an existing brand, product, or service. Voila! You have a positioning stance to own. So the next time, do not ask yourself 'how do I position my brand?'. Rather, ask yourselves, what am I un-positioning?' or 'who am I un-positioning?'.

Positioning is

said to be in place

only when the

consumer interprets

or decodes it,

and holds the thought

or the idea in his

mind.

FACET V

An asset or a liability?

Brand Property

Weak Association

A strong Property

Core

unstable Orbit

Brand properties make brands.

An asset or a liability?

Brand Property

As the word suggests, brand property is an asset, and sometimes, even a liability. In our lives, we as individuals tend to do things repeatedly, either consciously or subconsciously. Such actions get associated with us as our behaviour, preferences, tastes, habits, personalities etc., and before we know it, we begin to own them as our property. The trick is to know which of these associations should be possessed as assets, and which of these are needed to give up as liabilities. The same holds true in the world of brands.

If you smoke publically, the tag of a 'smoker' gets associated with you. If you are seen smoking more often, then it's possible that a tag of 'heavy smoker' is attached to you. Eventually, your identity, recognition, personality, or equity, could be that of a SMOKER, even if you are an artist or a policeman. Your 'smoker' association could become your brand property.

A brand could also own multiple properties. Let us observe a few examples where associations have become brand properties, and how a brand would cease to exist if it loses or gives up its brand property.

Imagine if Coca-Cola gave up its red colour. Poof! Coca-Cola will cease to exist as a brand. Why? Because the colour red associated with the brand is now an established brand property. Now imagine Pears soap as an opaque and rectangular soap, instead of being translucent and oval-shaped. The brand Pears will cease to exist. Similarly, Toblerone chocolates will cease to exist if they are coloured or pebble-shaped,

Brand Property

is an asset,
and sometimes,
even a liability.

or if Mini Cooper is marketed as an SUV, and the Land Rover as a sporty convertible.

The bottom line is, that brand properties make brands, and many times the essence of a brand is its brand property.

Even personalities have brand properties. Would you be able to relate to Napoleon Bonaparte without his signature hat, or to Hitler without his moustache? As mentioned earlier, brands have multiple brand properties. Mahatma Gandhi's brand properties would be his white loin cloth, thin skeletal body, round-rimmed glasses, a walking stick in his hand, and a bald head.

An effective brand strategy is to know which brand property to enhance or build the brand on, and which one to underplay or phase out.

Brand properties can be decoded by mapping out the various associations based on perceptions, experience, or even hearsay. (I suggest Interbrand's nodal mapping exercises, which give a clear pictorial map of associations). The interpretation of the mapping would clearly

spell out what a brand can do, what a brand should not do, what a brand could enhance, or how to spot the chink in the competition's armour.

Here is a crash course to identify your brand's property. If you do not own a brand, think about yourself as a brand, and this powerful mapping technique could give you some strategic direction for your life.

The association mapping can be done by asking the relevant audiences some simple, key questions like:

'When I say (name of brand), what comes to your mind first?'

'When I say (name of brand), what visuals come to your mind first?'

'When I say (name of brand), what words come to your mind first?'

'When I say (name of brand), what feelings come to your mind first?'

'When I say (name of brand), what other brands come to your mind first?'

'When I say (name of brand), why would somebody buy this brand?'

'When I say (name of brand), why would somebody not buy this brand?'

'When I say (name of brand), when, or on what occasion would somebody buy this brand?'

Make sure you have represented your relevant audience well. When you have all your responses, tabulate them by identifying common associations. Now, map the responses with greater numbers closer to the core of the map, and plot the lesser numbers further away from the core. The ones closer to the core will indicate that they are strong associations, asking you to consider them as brand properties to be enhanced or built on. The ones further away will tell you, that the association is yet to be established as a brand property, or if the association can be infringed on by a competitor. It could also warn you, if some unwanted association is close to the core of the brand, which could become a liability sooner or later.

Brand Association Mapping

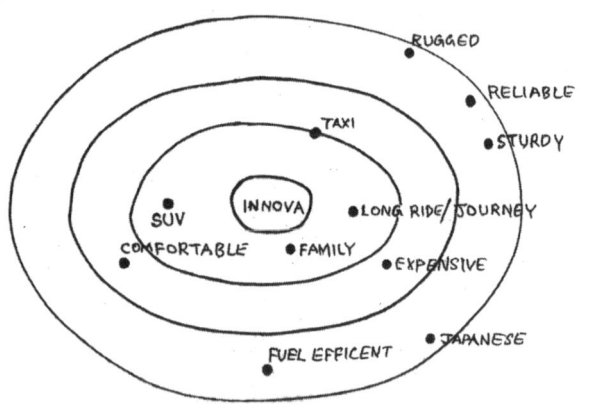

Here are some examples from my workshops, conducted among brand managers and senior advertising professionals. Let me begin with Toyota Innova, an SUV brand in India. On asking the participants the key association questions (as listed earlier), and mapping them, we derived some interesting responses, answering a few strategic questions (refer map):

What associations should Toyota Innova enhance or build on?

1. As a family SUV

2. Meant for long journeys

3. Comfortable

What associations should Toyota Innova be alert of, or look out for?

1. The danger of being positioned as a 'taxi', endangering the pride of ownership

2. The perception of being expensive

What associations should Toyota Innova not lose out on?

1. Fuel efficiency

2. Reliable and sturdy

3. Rugged use (as an SUV, this could play into the hands of the competition)

4. The pride of being a Japanese car

The exercise was useful to examine some strategic directions as a way forward for the brand.

Now, when you do a similar association mapping for the competition, you will be able to determine what associations or properties you should not infringe. You will also spot weak associations to take on the competition, making the brand strategy that's much more potent.

Brand associations and properties also play a crucial role in determining brand extensions and introduction of new variants into the market. Here are some interesting take-outs from some of my workshops:

Fanta in India was found to be associated strongly with orange flavour, orange colour, fun,

It could also

warn you if some

unwanted association

could become a

liability, sooner or later.

as a kid's fizz drink, for birthday parties, etc. But guess what?, when Fanta introduced an apple variant, the plan 'fizzled out' (excuse the pun).

Fanta had to be an orange drink in India, and it had to be a fun and frolic drink. Anything going against this meant an instant rejection, or an uphill marketing exercise, requiring enormous efforts to establish the new apple variant. It was never going to be easy to extend the brand Fanta in India, beyond an orange fizz drink. It was a clear case of a brand property becoming a liability, not allowing any further brand extensions.

Even more interesting was an exercise where the participants mapped the brand Pond's, in India. Pond's was found to be strongly associated with talcum powder, floral fragrance, face cream, purple and pink colours, used by women, usually dusted under the arms, etc.

Many years back, the owners/ custodians of the Pond's brand, thought, that it made immense sense to launch a Pond's toothpaste, and you know what? They actually launched it with some big ad spends. Now imagine all those associations in your mouth, first thing in the morning! Yes, that's how the consumers felt too. Yet, another case where brand properties became a liability, not allowing any further brand extensions.

Similarly Cadbury's associations with chocolates and chocolate flavour were so strong, that it was almost impossible to imagine strawberry flavoured milk from them. So, irrespective of how strong a brand is, its brand properties and associations could be a serious liability for its growth, or to beat the competition.

Here are some examples of brand extensions you could ponder upon:

1. An SUV from Volkswagen branded as a Beetle

2. Jockey as a formal blazer brand

3. Sony as a home lighting brand

4. A whiskey branded as Bud

5. The next James Bond movie by Pixar

Brand associations
and properties also
play a crucial role in
determining brand
extensions and
introduction of
new variants into
the market.

In many ways, isn't it the same when it comes to individuals? Our body shapes, sizes, our mannerisms, knowledge, dexterity, choice of clothes, the neighbourhood we come from, the car we drive, the style of communication, etc., all get associated with us, and eventually some become our brand properties for life. Are they assets or liabilities? Being aware of this will determine how well the brand is balanced.

Because, branding is like a bumpy bicycle ride.

FACET VI

How do I meet you next?

Brand Protocol

It's not about brand personality.
It's about brand presence, It's an
unwritten Code of conduct.

Rules are known
The protocol is known
The mission is known
The moves are expected

How do I meet you next?

Brand Protocol

Brand Protocol, as the word suggests, is about determining how the brand would address its consumers, especially the current and loyal consumers. When a consumer buys a product or service, s/he automatically begins to consume the brand's manners, customs, belief, its character, charisma, identity, temperament, personality, emotions, code of conduct, etc., not as a default, but as a conscious choice. A brand can build a lasting relationship or attract a new consumer, if it can strategically determine its protocol.

When a

consumer buys a

product or service, he

automatically begins to

consume the brand.

As we begin to decode this important facet of a brand, one begins to wonder how many of us appreciate the jargon, 'brand personality'. It is quite a popular jargon, used to articulate a brand in presentation slides or as a creative brief, by mentioning a set of three to four words, phrases or names of movie stars, or cars or restaurants. All is done with the belief, that the client or the creative guys in the advertising agency will somehow figure it out, or justify the articulation of brand personality in the brand's communication campaign.

While brand personality is more about the appearance, and the tone, and the manner of communication, brand protocol is about a code of conduct to be observed or maintained in the market. It is not just about the way a brand communicates, but the consistent manner in which the brand presents itself, maintaining a relationship, and allowing its customers to consume the brand, while they use the product. Brand protocol sets the engagement expectation, and the way in which the brand promise is delivered.

Brand Protocol

is about

a code of conduct

to be observed

or maintained in

the market.

Many a times, it is also an expectation, that a brand surprises its consumers with. But here again, the brand protocol needs to be maintained. The 'surprise' in its next appearance or engagement cannot contradict, misrepresent, or let down its consumers, with what the brand stands for, or what its personality is.

Let's take Eric Clapton, the legendary English blues and rock guitarist as an example. His fans come to his concert to hear him play serious blues and rock compositions, delivered in typical Clapton style, where he makes a gentlemanly entrance onto the stage, dressed in semi-formals, and letting his guitar do all the talking. That's the brand Eric Clapton, with its personality and its protocol fulfilled. He could surprise his fans by appearing in a tuxedo, making his appearance from the back of the audience. Now, if the brand Eric Clapton decides to make its appearance along with a punk rock band, yelling foul language, throwing up microphones in the air, and smashing guitars, then not only is the personality in question, but so is the the brand protocol.

Discounted premium brand

The brand protocol needs to determine where the brand needs to be present, which other brands will it be seen pitching against, which brands will it be seen with, what will be the tone and the manner of communication, and what values will it stand for in the eyes of its customers. These eventually need to be expressed, and made tangible and recognised, be it through packaging, advertising, events, communication channels, public relations, social media, etc.

The brand protocol sets an expectation for your next appearance or interaction with the brand. The next time you meet Coke, it will be dressed in red for sure, with an intention of spreading or sharing 'happiness' with you.

You can expect it and be assured, that the protocol would be adhered to. Similarly, you can expect the Ritz Hotel to address you by your surname, and offer you your favourite pillow-type, and wake you up with your preferred cup of tea, the next time you check-in to the hotel.

It is essential

that a brand protocol

doesn't contradict

or misrepresent

the brand's

positioning stance.

Let me walk you through another example. If I admire a brand of shirt as a premium , exclusive, apparel brand, and I find the brand's exclusive outlet being present on the fashion high street, the protocol that the brand holds with me is accepted and appreciated. Now, having bought the premium, exclusive brand from this outlet, if I then find it in a popular discount store later, it would mean that the brand has failed to hold its protocol with me, disrespecting my relationship with the brand.

Brand protocol is a well-determined expectation, created for the brand by its custodians or creators. If kids love visiting a brand of a fast food restaurant for its free surprise toy along with the meal, then this 'surprise toy' would be the way the brand holds its protocol with its young customers. That would be its custom or ritual of welcoming kids for a meal with a surprise toy. The day children fail to be surprised with a free toy, the protocol would break.

A brand's protocol becomes the first point of contact or reference for any consumer, and

One of the key

principles to

determine a

brand's protocol

is to ensure that none

of its audience is

discriminated.

hence, determining a brand's protocol demands clarity and responsibility. It is to be noted that a brand's protocol is rooted in a sound brand positioning stance. It is essential that a brand protocol doesn't contradict or misrepresent the brand's positioning stance.

Brand protocol would stand to be evaluated by its loyal consumer, or the prospective consumer, on the following key aspects:

1. Is the protocol relevant to me?

2. Is the protocol answering an emotional need?

3. Is the protocol taking me for granted, or is it respecting my taste and preferences?

4. Is the protocol being honest?

5. Is the protocol being consistent with what it claims to be?

When a brand re-positions itself in the market, it is only right that the brand protocol is also redefined. If an international music television channel enters India playing international hits, in line with its positioning stance, it is only correct

Brand protocol

could eventually

become a

brand property.

that it maintains its protocol as an international brand, featuring international artistes, and sponsoring Western or European acts and events. In the event of a strategic move to change its positioning stance to an Indian music brand for the Indian youth, it would demand, that the brand changes its protocol to be in line with the new positioning stance, now featuring Indian artistes, and sponsoring Indian and regional music acts.

A change in a brand's protocol needs to ensure that its audience or consumer is taken into confidence about the change in its positioning stance. In other words, a brand needs to seek permission from its consumers, before it changes its protocol. It could be in the form of a public relations campaign, an announcement, a teaser on its packaging, direct mailers, point of purchase, social media campaign, digital media, or as advertisements. An indication of acceptance could also be measured or assessed by a simple market study.

One of the key principles to determine a brand's protocol is to ensure that none of its audience is discriminated against. If a lower-end version of Mercedes Benz is introduced into the market at half the cost of the top-end model, the costumer for the lower-end model would expect the same protocol, as that of a top-end model customer, since he too is consuming the brand as much as the top-end customer. The showroom, the test drive ritual, courtesy calls, the walk-through, personal attendants, billing formalities, etc., all need to demonstrate, that the same protocol is maintained, respecting all its customers.

Here is another perspective to brand protocol. In most cases, a brand protocol could eventually become a brand property. A cookie outlet at the entrance of many malls in a city could eventually become an expectation from the brand over a period of time, making its presence at the entrance of malls as its brand property. The sign of becoming a brand property would be its absence felt by you, the moment you notice that you do not smell fresh cookies when you enter the mall. The protocol could also become the mall's protocol to welcome shoppers with fresh aroma of cookies.

Brand protocol is much like the relationship we hold with people and communities. We constantly set expectations, build reputations, attract admirations, command respect, and display uniqueness to differentiate. This we achieve by demonstrating tastes and preferences in acts, and participating in various engagements, showcasing calculated attitudes, and voicing choices with a clear and distinct personality.

In many ways, it seems that the determination of a brand protocol will eventually support or compliment a brand's purpose, its perspective, positioning, and properties.

Yes! brands

need to be aware of,
and hold their protocol,
because brands are
human too.

End Note

I now leave you with the decoded brand facets on 'what to say?', which I have shared with you in this book.

As this goes to the press, I have started decoding brand facets of 'how to say it?', which pertains to the execution of 'what to say?', that would ensure that a brand stays balanced.

I look forward to be associated with many more brands in the years to come, exploring and discovering the key facets of brands, to set them on track. I invite you to visit my website www.InsightsInsight.com

Trust this book was useful.

Disclaimer

The references to brands, corporate entities, or people, are based purely on secondary data, online data, information, quotes, and views. Although the author has made every effort to ensure that the information in this book was correct at the time of going to press, the author does not assume, and hereby disclaim any liability to any party for any loss, damage, or disruption caused by errors or omissions, whether such errors or omissions result from negligence, accident, or any other cause.

About The Author

PAVAN PADAKI

Brand practitioner and principal—Insights In Sight Consulting
Director-insights and creative, brand-comm

Popularly known as the Insight guru amongst his peers and clients, for his ability to make them see the unseen, Pavan practices the fine art of integrated marketing communication. With a rich experience of over 25 years in client management, research, account planning, creative and public relations, he specialises in discovering insights into the world of brands, creativity and business.

Pavan has trained over 200 brand managers and advertising professionals to apply key brand facets to their businesses and brands. As a professional, he helps corporates put their brands on track, by identifying and working on various brand dimensions.

He has engineered over 75 brands, by masterminding brands in terms of brand positioning, enhancing brand properties, and strategising and executing brand identities, and communication campaigns. He has scripted and executed over 50 TV commercials on air.

You could enrich and share your insights on successful brands, creativity and business, at: www.InsightsInsight.com, orchestrated by him.